Feel Good!

by Rachel Russ

OXFORD
UNIVERSITY PRESS

All About You

There is just one you!

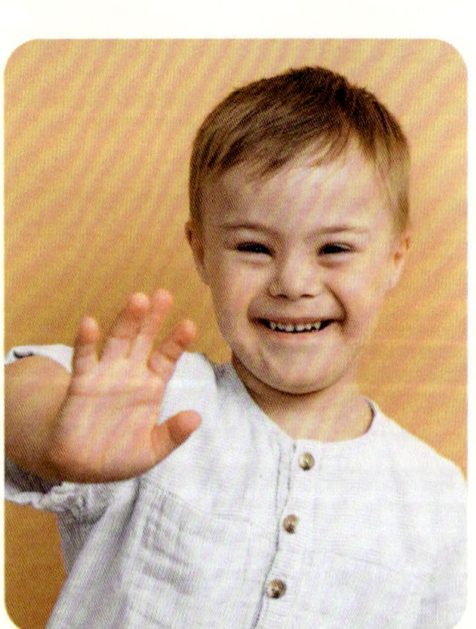

Lots of things can help you feel good.

Your Feelings

We all have different feelings.

It's normal to sometimes feel happy and sometimes feel sad. It can help to talk to someone you trust.

On The Go

Keeping fit is good for us.

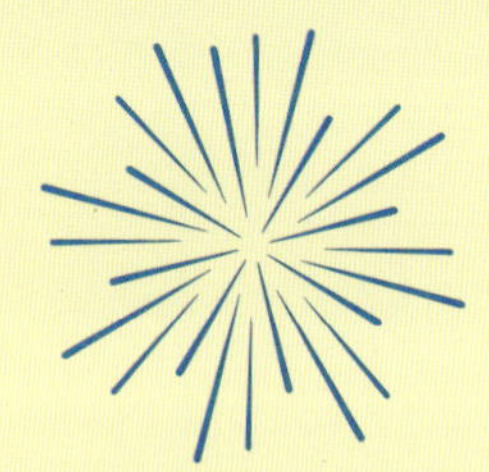

Swimming with my sister is fun.

When I run, I feel
the wind on my face.

Fresh Air

Many people enjoy spending time outside.

I like to spot birds when I walk.

It's fun to have a kick about.

Make Things

It can be relaxing to make things.

It's fun to bake.

I get a yummy treat, too!

Enjoy Yourself

Doing things we enjoy makes us feel good.

I love to make models.

Have a go at a new activity!

Eat Well

We need to eat well to keep well.

I like an apple
as a snack.

Breathing Deeply

Breathing deeply helps us to **relax**.

Have a go!

1. Breathing in,
   count to 3.

2. Keeping it in,
   count to 4.

3. Slowly breathing out,
   count to 5.

Chill Out

Pick an activity that makes you feel relaxed.

Hearing tunes I like helps me chill out.

Reading a book can take you to different places. Where will you go?

Sleep Tight

Good sleep helps us to keep well.

To sleep well, you should:

- go outside in the day
- do something that relaxes you
- go to bed at the same time.

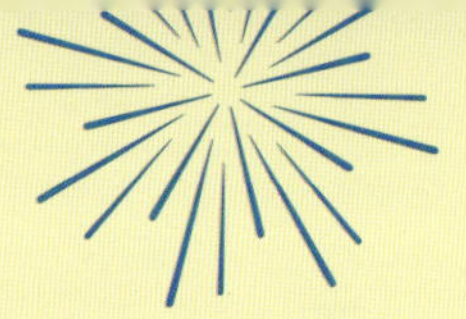

Talk About It

What do you do to have fun?

Who can you talk to about your feelings?

What do you do to feel good?

I take my dog for a walk.

What do you do to relax?

I like hearing Dad read my book!

Look It Up

proud: happy with something

relax: chill out

upset: feel sad

Index